discovermore
Good Health

Vitamins

Ursula Pang

Britannica Educational Publishing
IN ASSOCIATION WITH
THE ROSEN PUBLISHING GROUP

Published in 2027 by Britannica Educational Publishing (a trademark of Encyclopædia Britannica, Inc.) in association with The Rosen Publishing Group, Inc.
2544 Clinton Street, Buffalo, NY 14224

Distributed exclusively by Rosen Publishing.
To see additional Britannica Educational Publishing titles, go to rosenpublishing.com.

Editor: Greg Roza
Book Design: Michael Flynn

Photo Credits: Cover Tatjana Baibakova/Shutterstock.com; (series background) Dai Yim/Shutterstock.com; p. 4 Nomad_Soul/Shutterstock.com; p. 5 YARUNIV Studio/Shutterstock.com; p. 6 MattL_Images/Shutterstock.com; p. 7 brgfx/Shutterstock.com; p. 8 luchschenF/Shutterstock.com; p. 9 Saeedatun/Shutterstock.com; p. 10 Tatevosian Yana/Shutterstock.com; p. 11 Murilo Mazzo/Shutterstock.com; p. 12 Lapina/Shutterstock.com; p. 13 gemini2mars/Shutterstock.com; p. 14 Alexander Prokopenko/Shutterstock.com; p. 15 Art of Kosi/Shutterstock.com; p. 16 Tushar Pixart/Shutterstock.com; p. 17 Anatoliy Karlyuk/Shutterstock.com; p. 19 (top) Chernyshkova Natalia/Shutterstock.com; p. 19 (bottom) Tatjana Baibakova/Shutterstock.com; p. 20 lucky_pics/Shutterstock.com; p. 21 https://commons.wikimedia.org/wiki/File:A_case_of_Scurvy_journal_of_Henry_Walsh_Mahon.jpg; p. 22 3dMediSphere/Shutterstock.com; p. 23 Magic mine/Shutterstock.com; p. 24 Olena Rudo/Shutterstock.com; p. 25 New Africa/Shutterstock.com; p. 26 Inspiration GP/Shutterstock.com; p. 27 Rix Pix Photography/Shutterstock.com; p. 29 (top) PJ McDonnell/Shutterstock.com; p. 29 (bottom) Andy Shell/Shutterstock.com.

Cataloging-in-Publication Data

Names: Pang, Ursula.
Title: Vitamins / Ursula Pang.
Description: Buffalo, New York : Britannica Educational Publishing, an imprint of Rosen Publishing, 2027. | Series: Discover more: good health | Includes glossary and index.
Identifiers: ISBN 9781641905985 (pbk.) | ISBN 9781641905992 (library bound) | ISBN 9781641906005 (ebook)
Subjects: LCSH: Vitamins in human nutrition--Juvenile literature. | Vitamins--Juvenile literature. | Nutrition--Juvenile literature.
Classification: LCC TX553.V5 P36 2027 | DDC 612.399--dc23

Manufactured in the United States of America

CPSIA Compliance Information: Batch #CSBRIT27. For further information contact Rosen Publishing at 1-800-237-9932.

Contents

Essential for Health

People eat food to get nutrients in their daily diets. Vitamins are nutrients that humans need to grow, reproduce, and be healthy. They help to keep the systems of the body working properly. Each vitamin has specific roles to play. Many processes in the body require several vitamins. Too much or too little of one vitamin can interfere with the function of another.

Vitamins regulate many different functions of the body. Vitamins are very important for keeping people healthy.

Eating a variety of healthy foods, especially fruits and vegetables, allows us to get all the vitamins we need.

Scientists have identified thirteen vitamins that are **essential** for good health: A, C, D, E, and K, plus eight B vitamins. (Many vitamins have scientific names as well as their letter names.) Most of these vitamins can be obtained through a healthy diet filled with a variety of foods, including plenty of fruits and vegetables. Two vitamins—D and K—are made in the human body. Vitamins are needed in only small amounts, but a lack of any essential vitamin can cause health problems.

WORD WISE

THINGS THAT ARE ESSENTIAL ARE SO IMPORTANT THAT THEY HAVE TO BE INCLUDED.

Roles in the Human Body

Vitamins are not an energy source for the body like other nutrients are. They help to convert the other nutrients—carbohydrates, fats, and proteins—into energy. Vitamins also play a role in building tissues and regulating chemical activities.

There are two groups of vitamins: water soluble and fat soluble. Water-soluble vitamins include the B vitamins and vitamin C. They dissolve in water. The body stores a small amount of water-soluble vitamins, but it gets rid of most of those it does not use. Because of that, people must get a steady supply of those vitamins.

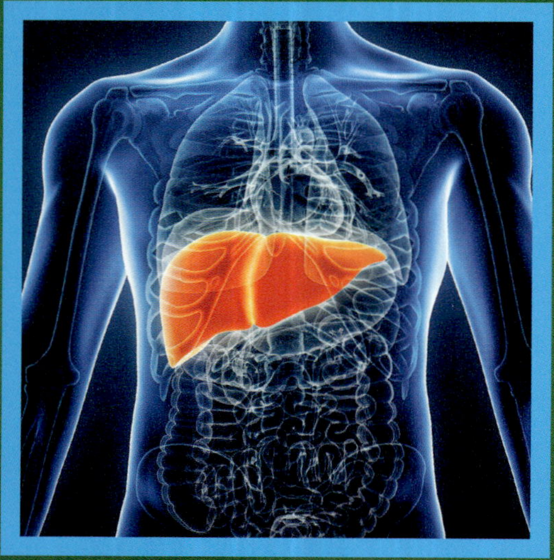

Fat-soluble vitamins include A, D, E, and K. They do not dissolve in water and are mostly stored in the body's fat and liver.

The liver is a large organ that has several important roles in our health, including storing nutrients such as vitamins and minerals.

We can easily get the daily requirements of vitamins we need by eating a wide variety of plant and animal foods.

Different amounts of each vitamin are recommended for men and women at different life stages. The daily amount of a nutrient that meets the needs of most healthy people is called the recommended dietary allowance (RDA).

Consider This

Why might it be useful for the body to store some vitamins?

A Look at Vitamin A

Vitamin A is a fat-soluble vitamin. It's also called retinol. Vitamin A is very important for good vision, but it also supports several other parts and functions of the body. These include the reproductive system, bone and tissue growth, and organs such as the heart and kidneys. In addition, vitamin A helps the body's immune system to fight off infections.

Beauty products with retinol in them are used to repair damaged skin and to treat acne.

Carrots are an excellent source of beta carotene, vitamin K1, fiber, and essential minerals. It's a low-calorie, low-fat, nutritious snack!

There are two types of dietary sources of vitamin A. Preformed vitamin A is found in animal products, such as liver, fish oils, dairy products, and eggs. Plants do not contain vitamin A, but some plant foods do provide vitamin A precursors. These are chemicals that the body can convert into vitamin A. Beta carotene, for example, is a vitamin A precursor found in carrots and other vegetables. Vitamin precursors are also called provitamins.

Consider This

A lot of orange vegetables and fruits contain beta carotene, which is turned into vitamin A in the body. Do you think any of your favorite vegetables or fruits are good sources of vitamin A?

A Look at Vitamin C

Vitamin C plays an important role in building and repairing connective tissue that is found in muscles, fat, and joints. For this reason, vitamin C helps to heal wounds. Vitamin C also supports the immune system and helps the body to absorb iron, an important mineral. In addition, vitamin C is an **antioxidant** that works to protect the body's cells from damage. People sometimes take extra vitamin C to fight off a cold, but scientific research has found that doing so is not very useful.

Vitamin C is a water-soluble vitamin also called ascorbic acid. Many fruits and vegetables are excellent sources of ascorbic acid.

Guava is a fruit that's very high in vitamin C. It's best eaten fresh!

Vitamin C is found in many fruits and vegetables, especially cantaloupe, citrus fruits, vegetables in the cabbage family, peppers, sweet potatoes, and leafy green vegetables. They yield the most vitamin C when eaten raw and fresh. The amount of vitamin C in fruits and vegetables can often be reduced by cooking and long storage.

WORD WISE

AN ANTIOXIDANT IS A SUBSTANCE THAT OPPOSES OXIDATION—REACTIONS MADE EASIER BY OXYGEN. IN THE BODY, ANTIOXIDANTS HELP TO PREVENT HARMFUL REACTIONS.

A Look at Vitamin D

Vitamin D is a fat-soluble vitamin. It is essential for growing and maintaining healthy bones. Vitamin D helps the body absorb calcium, the mineral that makes up bones. It also performs other jobs throughout the body. It promotes healthy muscles, supports the immune system, and helps the nervous system carry messages. Vitamin D also may help protect against some types of cancer.

When sunlight hits your skin, it makes vitamin D from cholesterol in your skin cells. Cholesterol is a fat known as a lipid.

Common vitamin D fortified foods include cow milk, plant-based milks, breakfast cereals, and orange juice.

The body makes vitamin D when the skin is directly exposed to sunlight. People who experience little sun exposure and people with dark skin may not produce enough vitamin D for the body's needs. Therefore, it is important to get vitamin D through the diet, too.

There are very few foods that naturally contain vitamin D. The best sources are certain types of fish, such as salmon and tuna. Most dietary vitamin D comes from foods that are fortified with vitamin D, which means the vitamin is added to them by food manufacturers.

Consider This

Can you explain why vitamin D is called the "sunshine vitamin"?

A Look at Vitamins E and K

Vitamin E is a fat-soluble vitamin. It functions mostly as an antioxidant in the body. Vitamin E protects the cells of the body from damage that contributes to disease and aging. Scientists do not fully understand the role of vitamin E in the body. Good sources of vitamin E include vegetable oils, nuts, seeds, and green vegetables.

Avocados are another good source of vitamin E.

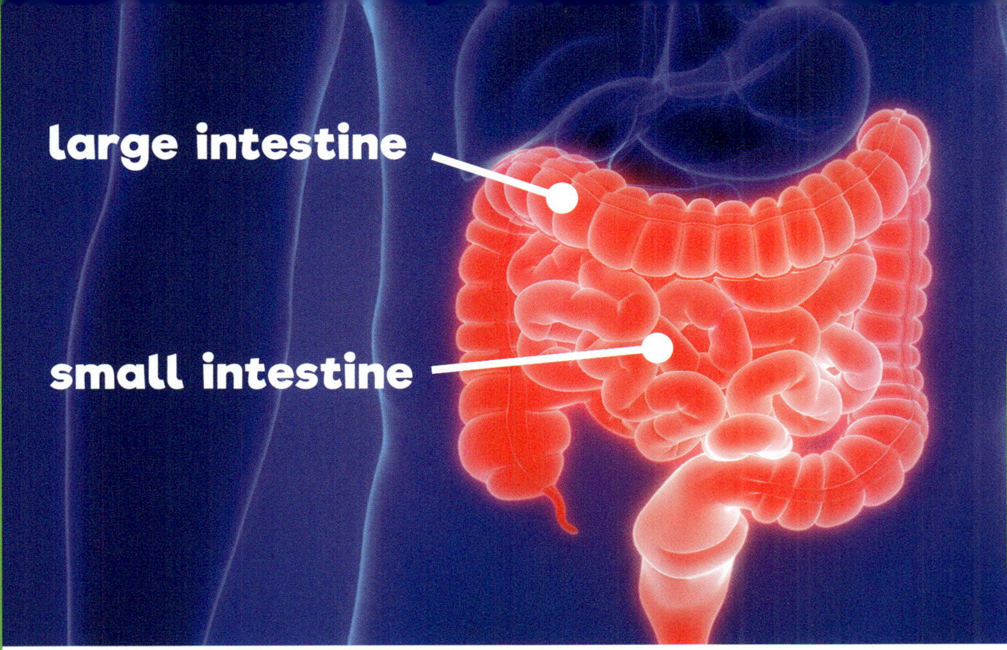

Bacteria in the intestines make most of the vitamin K that people require.

Vitamin K, another fat-soluble vitamin, enables blood to clot. Without vitamin K, even a small cut might not stop bleeding. Vitamin K is also important for bone health. There are two forms of vitamin K. Plants also produce a form of vitamin K. Green leafy vegetables, vegetable oils, and certain fruits such as blueberries all provide vitamin K. Blueberries are sometimes called a "superfood" for their nutritional value, which includes numerous vitamins and minerals.

Consider This

Medicines called antibiotics can kill bacteria in the digestive system. Why might a long course of antibiotics decrease the amount of vitamin K being produced in the body?

A Look at the B Vitamins

There are eight different B vitamins that are all water soluble. The entire group is sometimes called vitamin B complex. The B vitamins are not all related chemically to one another. However, they perform similar functions and are often found in the same food sources.

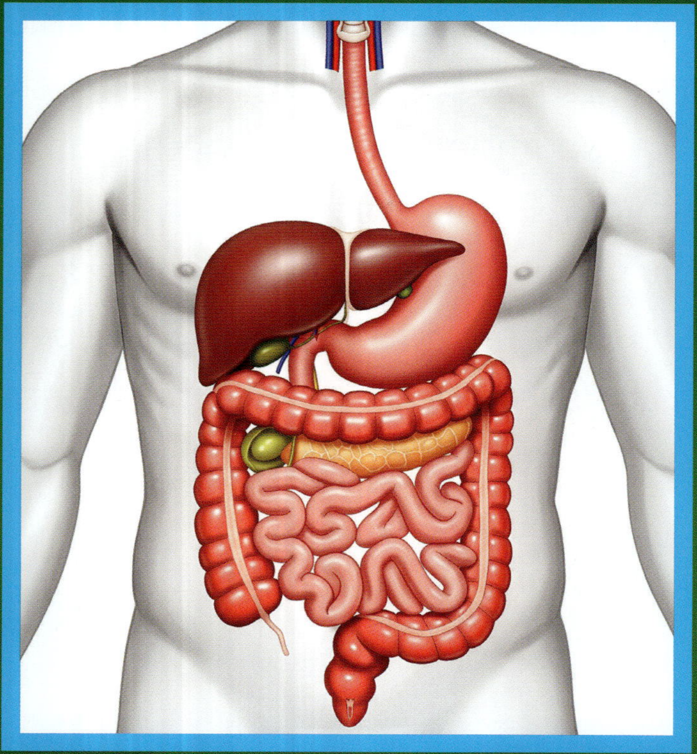

B vitamins give the body energy as food is broken down in the digestive system.

Recent studies have shown that riboflavin can help ease the symptoms, or signs, or migraine headaches.

Vitamin B_1 (also called thiamin), vitamin B_2 (riboflavin), and vitamin B_3 (niacin) are all involved in the **metabolism** of carbohydrates. This means that they help to break down carbohydrates and convert them into energy. They all play specific roles in supporting the healthy growth and function of certain cells in the body.

WORD WISE

METABOLISM IS THE COMBINED CHEMICAL REACTIONS THAT KEEP LIVING CELLS HEALTHY. THE REACTIONS INVOLVE BUILDING UP OR BREAKING DOWN SUBSTANCES CALLED MOLECULES SO A LIVING BODY CAN GET ENERGY, GROW, HEAL, AND GET RID OF WASTE MATERIAL.

Other B vitamins have more specific jobs. For example, vitamin B_6 helps to metabolize proteins. It also plays many other important roles. It contributes to making some of the chemicals that transmit messages in the brain. Vitamin B_6 also supports the immune system.

Vitamin B_9 is more often called folic acid or folate. It is important in making DNA, a chemical found inside every cell. DNA carries information about a person's physical traits.

Vitamin B_{12} cooperates with folic acid in producing DNA. Vitamin B_{12} also helps to produce red blood cells and supports the nervous system. Unlike other B vitamins, vitamin B_{12} is found only in animal foods such as beef, fish, eggs, and dairy products.

Vitamin B_5 (pantothenic acid) and vitamin B_7 (biotin) both support metabolism. They are important for overall growth and good health.

B vitamins can be found in a variety of dietary sources. Foods that contain significant amounts of various B vitamins include green vegetables, whole grains, legumes, seeds, nuts, meat, fish, eggs, and dairy products.

Leafy green vegetables are good sources of B vitamins. Other significant sources include salmon, liver, eggs, and legumes.

compareandcontrast

Some vegetarians eat dairy and eggs, while others, called vegans, consume no animal products. Which group should be more concerned about getting enough vitamin B12?

B12 is mostly found in animal foods, particularly red meat. The vitamin is also added to some foods such as cereal.

What's a Deficiency?

A deficiency is a lack of something. A vitamin deficiency is a lack of an essential vitamin. This can cause serious health problems, and deficiencies of certain vitamins result in specific diseases.

Vitamin A deficiency can lead to vision problems. An early sign of a vitamin A deficiency is night blindness—not being able to see in dim light or at night. Severe, lifelong vitamin A deficiency can cause lasting blindness. Other health effects include weak bones, very dry skin, and a weakened immune system.

One sign of vitamin A deficiency is night blindness. This condition can make driving at night difficult and even dangerous.

These illustrations of the affects of scurvy were created around 1841 by a British surgeon while aboard a ship taking convicts from England to Australia.

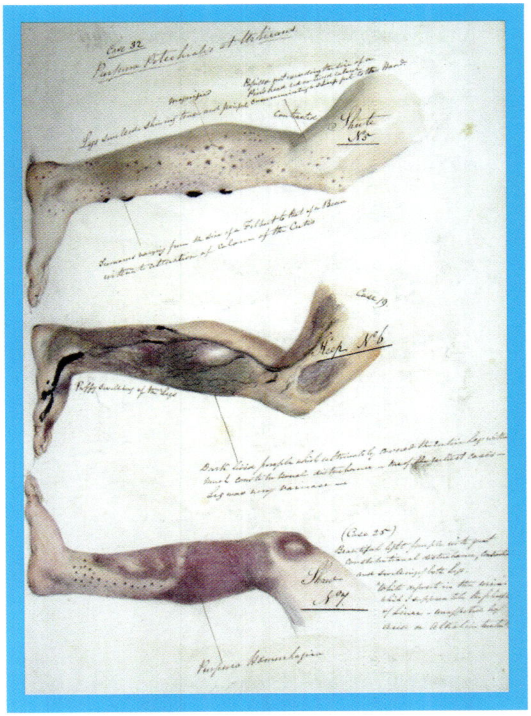

Severe vitamin C deficiency can cause a disease called scurvy. Scurvy is marked by weakness, joint pain, and bleeding gums. In past centuries, sailors on long voyages often suffered from scurvy because they did not have access to fresh fruits and vegetables.

Vitamin D deficiency can result in a disease called rickets in children. This condition causes bone problems such as bowed legs and slow growth. Older adults with a vitamin D deficiency have a risk of bone problems such as osteoporosis, a condition where bones become weak and break easily.

Consider This

People of different ages require different amounts of vitamins, but kids should get as much vitamin D as adults. Why do you think vitamin D is so important for children's health?

B vitamin deficiencies can result in several different diseases. Vitamin B_1 (thiamin) deficiency can cause beriberi. Symptoms include muscle weakness, tingling and numbness in fingers and toes, and mental symptoms such as confusion. A severe vitamin B_3 (niacin) deficiency can lead to pellagra, a possibly fatal disease. Diarrhea, dermatitis (skin problems), and dementia (a mental illness) are symptoms of pellagra.

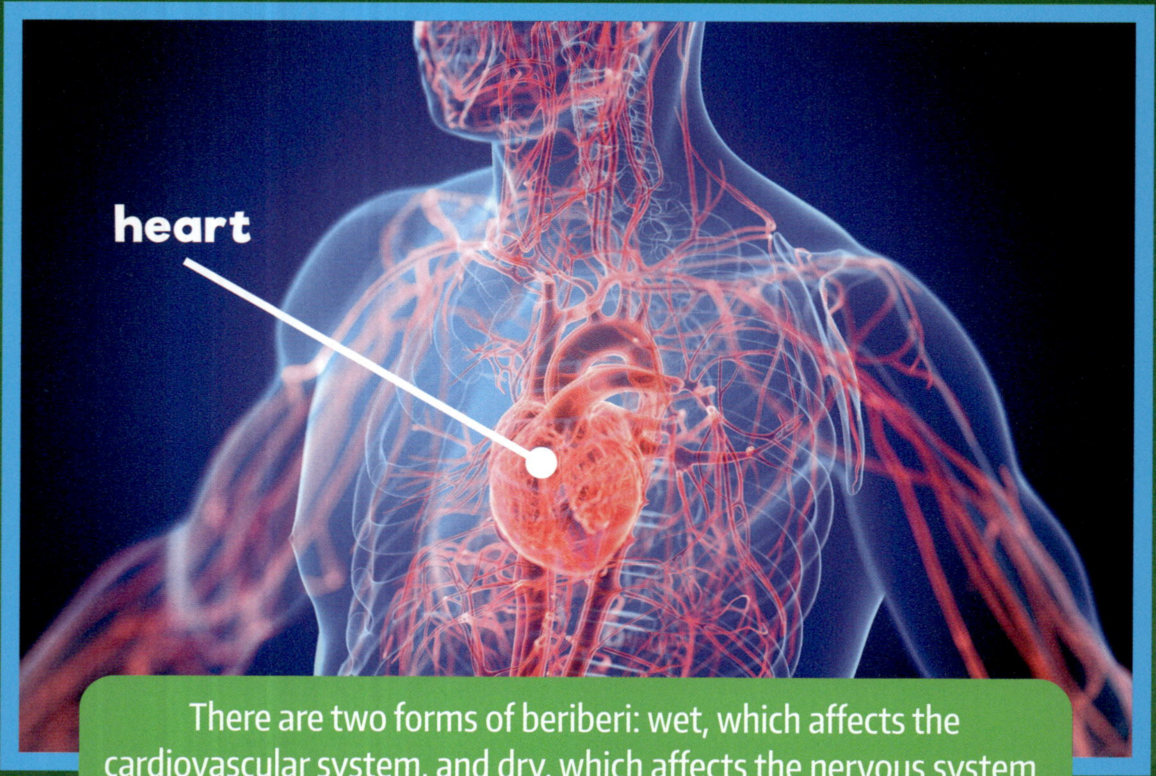

There are two forms of beriberi: wet, which affects the cardiovascular system, and dry, which affects the nervous system. Both can be treated with thiamin-rich foods and medications.

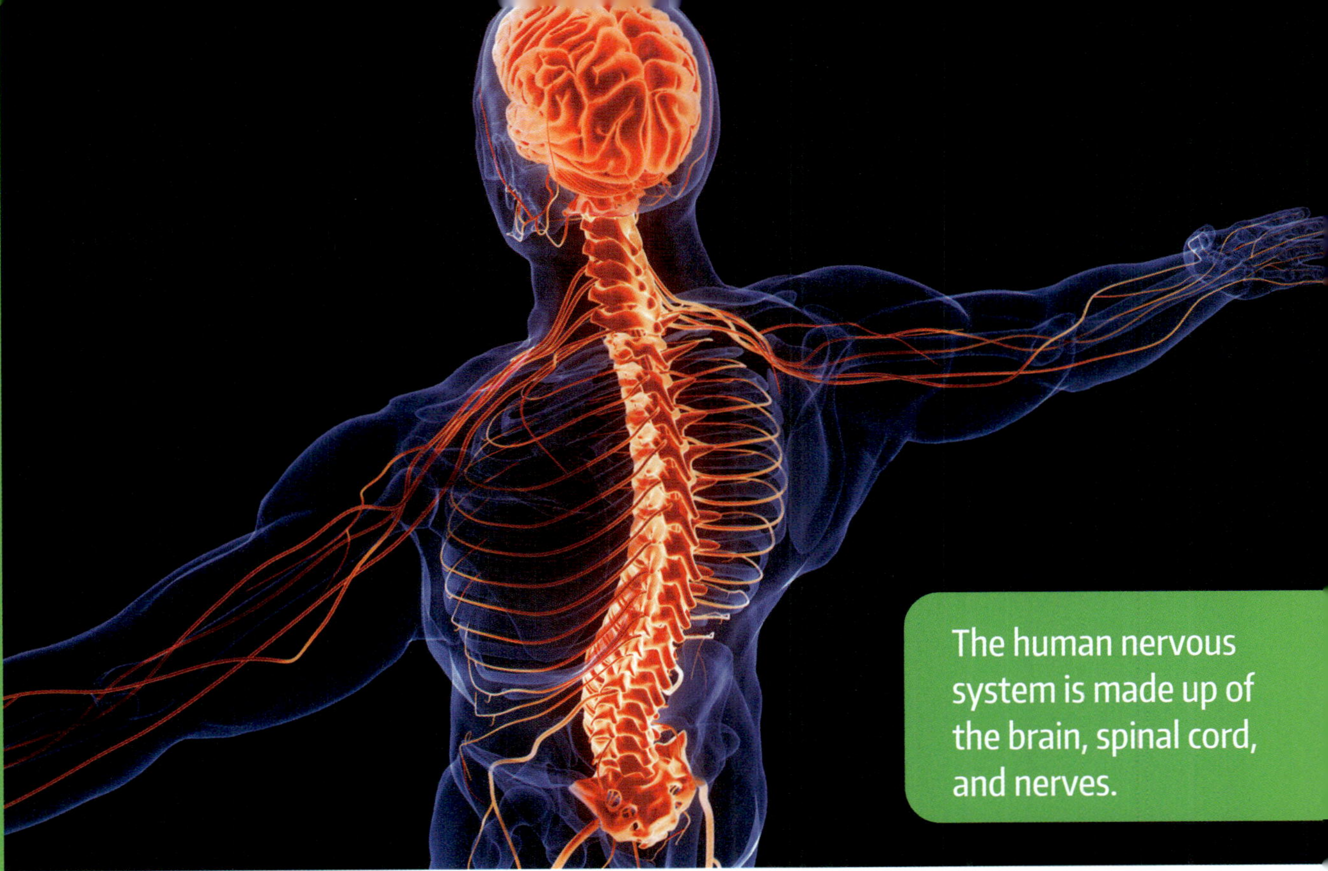

The human nervous system is made up of the brain, spinal cord, and nerves.

Folic acid deficiency and vitamin B_{12} deficiency often cause similar symptoms. They both can result in a type of **anemia** that leaves people feeling weak and tired. Vitamin B_{12} deficiency also can cause problems with the nervous system.

WORD WISE

ANEMIA IS A CONDITION IN WHICH A PERSON HAS FEWER RED BLOOD CELLS THAN NORMAL. IT CAN LEAD TO WEAKNESS, PALE SKIN, SHORTNESS OF BREATH, AND AN UNEVEN HEARTBEAT.

Too Many Vitamins!

It's never a good idea to take more medication than your doctor recommends, and that includes vitamins as well. For some vitamins, doses above the RDA can be dangerous. This danger is especially true of fat-soluble vitamins, which can be stored in the body. If large amounts build up, they can lead to **toxicity**. In general, children are more vulnerable to vitamin overdose than adults.

Children's vitamins often look like candy, but it's important to take the recommend amount to avoid health problems.

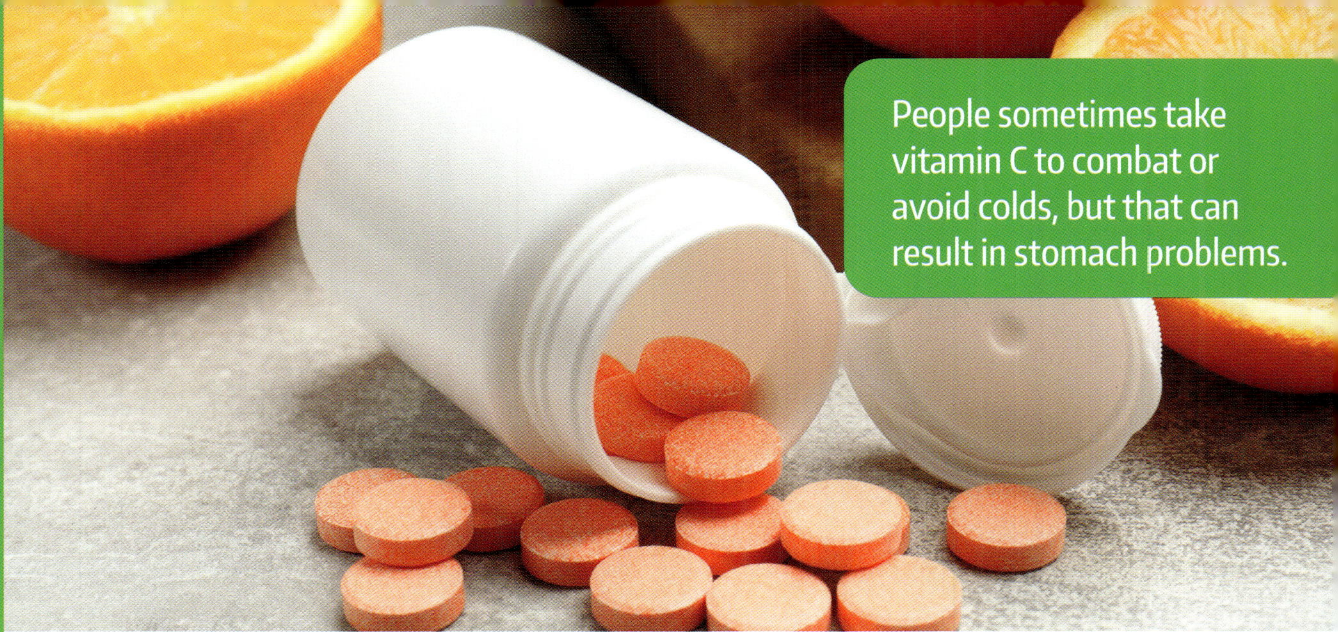

People sometimes take vitamin C to combat or avoid colds, but that can result in stomach problems.

Too much vitamin A can cause stomach distress, unhealthy skin and hair, bone pain, headaches, and blurred vision. Liver damage from vitamin A toxicity can be permanent. Too much vitamin D can cause weakness and nausea. An excess of vitamin D also can damage the kidneys.

Severe health problems from water-soluble vitamins are rare. But overdoses can have short-term consequences. For example, too much vitamin B_3 (niacin) causes reddened skin. To much vitamin C can cause an upset stomach.

WORD WISE

VITAMIN TOXICITY IS A CONDITION IN WHICH A PERSON DEVELOPS HARMFUL SYMPTOMS AS A RESULT OF TAKING LARGE DOSES OF VITAMINS.

Reading Food Labels

Healthy meals should include a variety of nutritious foods. This usually supplies all the vitamins a person needs every day. The amounts of vitamins required daily is very small. They are measured in units called milligrams or even micrograms. Trying new foods and combining them in different ways can make getting vitamins fun.

This is a great example of a well-balanced lunch loaded with essential vitamins.

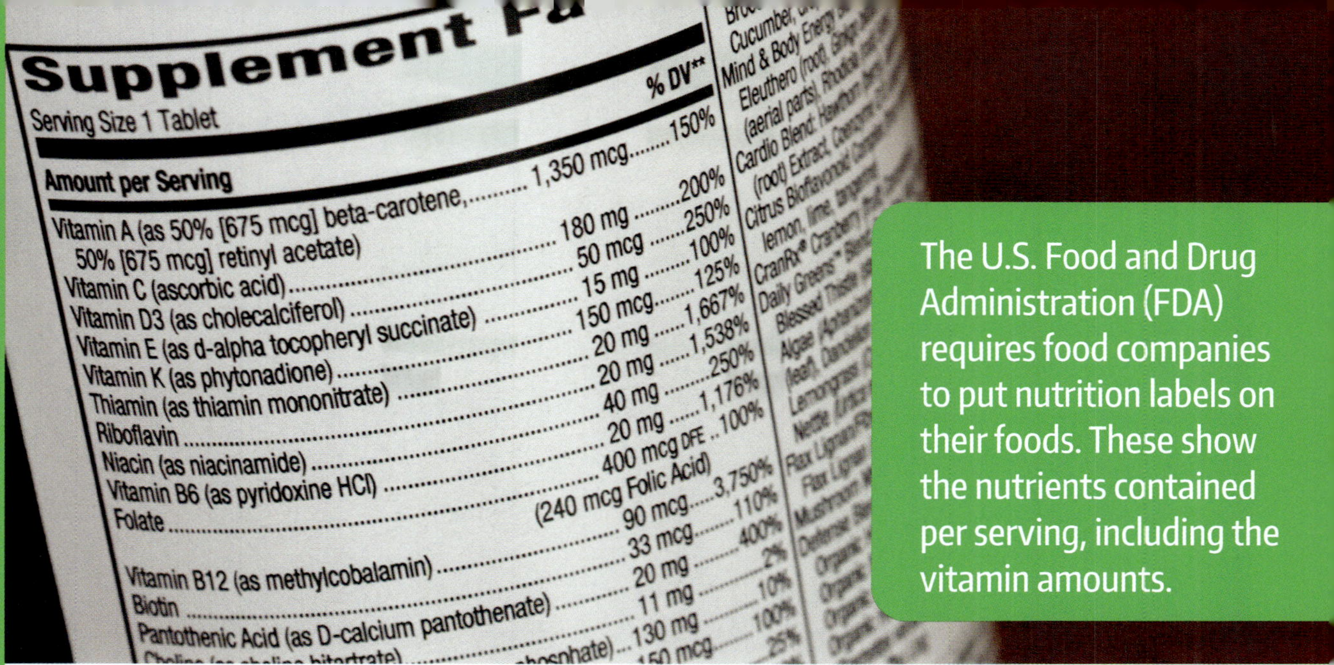

The U.S. Food and Drug Administration (FDA) requires food companies to put nutrition labels on their foods. These show the nutrients contained per serving, including the vitamin amounts.

To prevent vitamin deficiencies, food companies sometimes add vitamins to products. This process is called food fortification. Milk is fortified with vitamin D. Cereal is often fortified with a variety of vitamins and minerals. The nutritional information on a food label shows the amounts of vitamins found in the food, both naturally occurring and fortified. Online government databases list the nutrients in thousands of different foods.

Consider This

In the past, the disease pellagra, caused by a deficiency of niacin, was common in the United States. Since the mid-twentieth century, pellagra has become very rare. Why do you think that might be?

Vitamin Supplements

Vitamin supplements provide an extra dose of one or more vitamins. Supplements come in different forms, including pills, chewables, liquids, and gummies. They may include a single vitamin or many vitamins packaged into a multivitamin.

Most healthy people do not need vitamin supplements. But certain people may have a higher risk of vitamin deficiency. People who restrict their diets, such as vegetarians, may have trouble getting the required levels of some vitamins. Some medications can make vitamins less effective. Women who are pregnant may need to take vitamin supplements to guarantee that babies are born healthy.

Some people believe that extra vitamins will improve their health, but it doesn't always work like that. It is very rare for someone to overdose on vitamins through diet alone. Vitamin supplements, however, can provide huge doses in a single pill that could have harmful results.

Vitamin supplements are a big business! Look at all the supplements in this store.

compareandcontrast

What are the benefits of taking vitamin supplements? What are the possible problems?

For some people, vitamin supplements or multivitamins may be recommended in addition to eating a healthy diet.

Glossary

absorb To take in or swallow up.
cell One of the tiny units that are the basic building blocks of living things.
cholesterol A waxy substance present in animal cells that is important in bodily processes.
diet The food and drink that a person, animal, or group takes in.
disease An abnormal bodily condition that interferes with functioning and can usually be recognized by signs and symptoms.
fortify The act of making something stronger, or the addition of material to something for strengthening or improving it.
function The natural action of a part in a living thing.
immune system The parts of the body that protect it from foreign substances, such as germs.
legume A type of plant, such as a pea or bean plant, with seeds that grow in long cases called pods and are used for food.
mineral In nutrition, matter that is not plant or animal material, that is necessary for good health, and that is obtained from food.
muscle A body tissue consisting of long cells that can contract and produce movement.
nervous system The collection of nerves that send messages for controlling movement and feeling between the brain and the other parts of the body.
nutrients Substances that plants, animals, and people need to live and grow.
organ A part of a person, plant, or animal that consists of cells and tissues and is specialized to do a particular task.
overdose To take too much of a drug, medicine, or other substance at one time.
precursor A substance from which another substance is formed by natural processes.
reproductive system The body parts that allow animals to create babies.
restrict To place under limits as to use.
supplement Something that supplies what is needed or makes an addition.
tissue In the body, a mass or layer of cells, usually of one kind.
trait An inherited characteristic.
vulnerable Capable of being wounded; open to attack or damage.

For More Information

Books

Kuehl, Ashley. *Nutrition*. Bloomington MN: SilverTip Books, 2025.

Slingerland, Janet. *Vitamins*. Mendota Heights, MN: North Star Editions, 2024.

Websites

How to Make Healthy Food Choices
kidshealth.org/en/kids/pyramid.html
Read all about nutrition and find links to similarly related topics.

How to Understand and Use the Nutrition Facts Label
www.fda.gov/food/nutrition-facts-label/how-understand-and-use-nutrition-facts-label
Read more about food labels and how to use them at this detailed website from the FDA.

Index